$\mathcal{T}$his book records the
Thanksgiving Memories
of the

———————————————————

Family

Give thanks to the LORD, for he is good;
his love endures forever.

Psalm 107:1

Love and prayers,
Dad & Elsie

May God bless you and give you Thanksgivings filled with rich memories and heartfelt celebrations that you will cherish always.

We Give
Thanks

A Thanksgiving Keepsake Book

ZondervanPublishingHouse

Grand Rapids, Michigan

A Division of HarperCollinsPublishers

We Give Thanks
A Thanksgiving Keepsake Book

Copyright ©1996 by The Zondervan Corporation

ISBN 0-310-96790-2

Requests for information should be addressed to:
   ⛪ Zondervan Publishing House
      Grand Rapids, Michigan 49530

Printed in The United States of America

Project Editors: Joy L. Marple & Cara Bailey
Art Directors: Patricia Matthews & Mark Veldheer
Illustrators: Robin Moro & Rick Jacobi

Table of Contents

*T*hanksgiving is a special holiday when families and friends gather to give thanks to the Lord. This keepsake book is designed to enrich your Thanksgiving celebration by providing a place to record your blessings and memories.

🍎 *Share a thankful prayer.*

🍎 *Sing a favorite hymn or two.*

🍎 *Read the Thanksgiving story.*

🍎 *Recite poetry and Scripture together as you gather around the table.*

🍎 *Take a candid photo as a keepsake of the family and friends who gather each year to share in the celebration.*

🍎 *Record the names of loved ones who are present each Thanksgiving.*

🍎 *Pass the book around the table asking each person to write what they are thankful for that year. Then look and reflect on how God has blessed your family and friends from one generation to the next.*

🍎 *Write your favorite recipes in the back of the book so you have a convenient place to locate them year after year.*

Many of these ideas will help you focus on the blessings of this holiday. Use this keepsake book to help make your Thanksgiving celebration a more memorable, enjoyable and exciting holiday for you and those you love.

The First Thanksgiving

Many years ago, 1607 to be exact, a group of English people known as Separatists left England because they were not able to worship God in the way they thought they should. They decided to emigrate to Holland to establish a new religious community—one where they would be able to worship the way they wanted. They looked forward to living in a country that would not tell them how to worship. When they arrived in Holland, they were surprised to find how difficult it was for them to adjust to the Dutch life-style. One problem was that they did not know the language. Another problem was that while in England they worked as farmers, but in Holland they had to work in factories because those were the only jobs available to them. They stayed in Holland for twelve years but then decided that their life there was not any better than the life they had left in England. They decided to leave Holland. And they decided not to return to England either! They decided to go to the New World—the land of opportunity and plenty!

In July 1620, forty-six Separatists boarded the Speedwell, the ship that would carry them away from Holland and to their new lives! Their first stop was Southampton, England where they planned to join the Mayflower, the other ship with which they would travel. Following many delays, they discovered that the Speedwell would not be able to complete the long ocean voyage to America. Most of the Separatists, however, were able to join the English colonists on the Mayflower. On September 6 they all left England and headed for America.

The Pilgrims were very excited when after 98 days of sailing, they landed at Plymouth, Massachusetts. Their excitement soon turned to sorrow, however, when the hard winter began to take its toll. During the first

(Continued on page 10)

(Continued from page 8)

bitter winter in the New World, 47 Pilgrims died because of illness and disease. Thankfully, Squanto, a local Wampanoag Indian, provided the remaining 55 Pilgrims with help that allowed them to survive. With his help, the Pilgrims learned to hunt, fish, and build houses. When the weather improved, he taught them to plant crops of corn and squash. Squanto also proved to be a valuable friend when he served as negotiator and interpreter between the Pilgrims and the Indians. Several years before the Pilgrims arrived in America, Squanto had been captured by English fishermen. It was during that time that he learned to speak English.

After their first successful harvest, the Pilgrim's Governor, William Bradford, announced that they would hold a Thanksgiving celebration. The Pilgrims began to make plans for their joyous celebration. They decided to show their appreciation to the Indians by inviting Massasoit, chief of the Wampanoags, to their celebration. Massasoit and 90 of his braves gladly accepted their invitation. The Pilgrims and the Indians had a wonderful time together—complete with games and a demonstration of their weapons. When they sat down together, they feasted on duck, goose, seafood, eels, cornbread, greens, pumpkins, wild plums and dried berries. The Indians provided several deer for the feast. All of the food was prepared and served by only four women and two teenage girls, the only women who had lived through the harsh winter. Compared to the previous winter, the Pilgrims were very thankful that they were able to participate in such a glorious celebration.

The Thanksgiving of 1621 was celebrated with excitement and enthusiasm but it was not until 1623 that there was another Thanksgiving celebration. Many people consider the celebration in 1623 to be the first Thanksgiving because it consisted of prayer and thanksgiving—more in line with the Puritan values of the Pilgrims. It was not until 1626 that Thanksgiving became an annual holiday.

"Our harvest being gotten in, our Govenour sent foure men fowling, so that we might after a more special manner rejoyce together, after we had gathered the fruit of our labours, they foure in one day killed as much fowle, as with a little helpe beside, served the Company almost a weeke, at which time, amongst other Recreations we exercized our Armes, many of the Indians coming amongst us, and amongst the rest their greatest King Massasoyt, with some ninetie men, whom for three days we entertained and feasted, and they went out and killed five Deere which they brought to the Plantacion and bestowed on our Govenour, and upon the Captaine, and others."

Edward Winslow, 1621

Thanksgiving Poetry

Every Day Thanksgiving Day

Sweet it is to see the sun
    Shining on Thanksgiving Day,
Sweet it is to see the snow
    Fall as if it came to stay;
Sweet is everything that comes,
    For all makes cheer, Thanksgiving Day.

Fine is the pantry's goodly store,
    And fine the heaping dish and tray;
Fine the church-bells ringing; fine
    All the dinners' great array,
Things we'd hardly dare to touch,
    Were it not Thanksgiving Day.

Dear the people coming home,
    Dear glad faces long away,
Dear the merry cries, and dear
    All the glad and happy play.
Dear the thanks, too, that we give
    For all of this Thanksgiving Day.

But sweeter, finer, dearer far
    It well might be if on our way,
With love for all, with thanks to Heaven,
    We did not wait for time's delay,
But, with remembered blessings then
    Made every day Thanksgiving Day.

Harriet Prescott Spofford

Thanksgiving Day

Brave and high-souled Pilgrims,
    you who knew no fears,
How your words of thankfulness
    go ringing down the years;
May we follow after; like you,
    work and pray,
And with hearts of thankfulness keep
Thanksgiving Day.

Annette Wynne

Landing of the Pilgrim Fathers

The breaking waves dashed high
On a stern and rockbound coast,
And the woods against a stormy sky
Their giant branches tossed;

And the heavy night hung dark
The hills and waters o'er,
When a band of exiles moored their bark
On the wild New England shore.

What sought they thus far?
Bright jewels of the mine?
The wealth of seas? the spoils of war?
They sought a faith's pure shrine!

Aye, call it holy ground,
The soil where first they trod:
They have left unstained what there they found—
Freedom to worship God!

Felicia Hemans

Harvest Hymn

Once more the liberal year laughs out
    O'er richer stores than gems or gold;
Once more with harvest-song and shout
    Is Nature's bloodless triumph told.

Oh, favors every year made new!
    Oh, gifts with rain and sunshine sent!
The bounty overruns our due,
    The fullness shames our discontent.

We shut our eyes, the flowers bloom on;
    We murmur, but the corn-ears fill,
We choose the shadow, but the sun
    That casts it shines behind us still.

Who murmurs at his lot today?
    Who scorns his native fruit and bloom?
Or sighs for dainties far away,
    Beside the bounteous board of home?

Thank Heaven, instead, that Freedom's arm
    Can change a rocky soil to gold,—
That brave and generous lives can warm
    A clime with northern ices cold.

And let these altars, wreathed with flowers
    And piled with fruits, awake again
Thanksgivings for the golden hours,
    The early and the latter rain!

John Greenleaf Whittier

The Pilgrims Came

The Pilgrims came across the sea,
        And never thought of you and me;
And yet it's very strange the way
        We think of them Thanksgiving Day.

We tell their story old and true
        Of how they sailed across the blue,
And found a new land to be free
        And built their homes quite near the sea.

Every child knows well the tale
        Of how they bravely turned the sail,
And journeyed many a day and night,
        To worship God as they thought right.

The people think that they were sad,
        And grave; I'm sure that they were glad—
They made Thanksgiving Day—that's fun—
        We thank the Pilgrims, every one!

        Annette Wynne

The Pumpkin

What moistens the lip and what brightens the eye?
What calls back the past like rich pumpkin pie?

        John Greenleaf Whittier

Thanksgiving Scripture Readings

Shout for joy to the LORD, all the earth.
Worship the LORD with gladness;
come before him with joyful songs.
Know that the LORD is God.
It is he who made us, and we are his;
we are his people, the sheep of his pasture.

Enter his gates with thanksgiving
and his courts with praise;
give thanks to him and praise his name.
For the LORD is good and his love endures forever;
his faithfulness continues through all generations.

Psalm 100

I will give thanks to the LORD because of his
righteousness and will sing praise to the name of
the LORD Most High.

Psalm 7:17

From the fullness of his grace we have all
received one blessing after another.

John 1:16

Come, let us sing for joy to the LORD;
let us shout aloud to the Rock of our salvation.
Let us come before him with thanksgiving
and extol him with music and song.

For the LORD is the great God,
the great King above all gods.
In his hand are the depths of the earth,
and the mountain peaks belong to him.
The sea is his, for he made it,
and his hands formed the dry land.

Come, let us bow down in worship,
let us kneel before the LORD our Maker;
for he is our God
and we are the people of his pasture,
the flock under his care.

Psalm 95:1–7

Give thanks to the LORD, for he is good; his love
endures forever.

Psalm 118:29

Give thanks to the LORD, call on his name;
make known among the nations what he has done.
Sing to him, sing praise to him;
tell of all his wonderful acts.
Glory in his holy name;
let the hearts of those who seek the LORD rejoice.
Look to the LORD and his strength;
seek his face always.
Remember the wonders he has done,
his miracles, and the judgments he pronounced.

1 Chronicles 16:8–12

The LORD is my strength and my shield;
    My heart trusts in him, and I am helped.
My heart leaps for joy
    and I will give thanks to him in song.

Psalm 28:7

Be joyful always; pray continually; give thanks in
all circumstances, for this is God's will for you in
Christ Jesus.

1 Thessalonians 5:16–18

Give thanks to the Lord, for he is good.
His love endures forever.
Give thanks to the God of gods.
His love endures forever.
Give thanks to the Lord of lords:
His love endures forever.
to him who alone does great wonders,
His love endures forever.
who by his understanding made the heavens,
His love endures forever.
who spread out the earth upon the waters,
His love endures forever.
who made the great lights—
His love endures forever.
the sun to govern the day,
His love endures forever.
the moon and stars to govern the night;
His love endures forever.
and who gives food to every creature.
His love endures forever.
Give thanks to the God of heaven.
His love endures forever.

Psalm 136:1–9,25–26

O Lord my God, I will give you thanks forever.

Psalm 30:12

Favorite Hymns of Thanksgiving

We Gather Together

We gather together to ask the Lord's blessing;
He chastens and hastens His will to make known;
The wicked oppressing now cease from distressing,
Sing praises to His Name: He forgets not His own.

Beside us to guide us, our God with us joining,
Ordaining, maintaining His kingdom divine;
So from the beginning the fight we were winning:
Thou, Lord, wast at our side, all glory be Thine!

We all do extol Thee, Thou Leader triumphant,
And pray that Thou still our Defender wilt be.
Let Thy congregation escape tribulation:
Thy Name be ever praised! O Lord, make us free! *Amen.*

This song, which celebrates the freedom of the Netherlands from a century of Spanish domination, was written by an unknown Dutch patriot. It was first published in a collection of Dutch songs in 1626. It was later translated into English by Theodore Baker.

We Plow the Fields, and Scatter

We plow the fields, and scatter
The good seed on the land,
But it is fed and watered
By God's almighty hand;
He sends the snow in winter,
The warmth to swell the grain,
The breezes and the sunshine,
And soft refreshing rain.

He only is the Maker
Of all things near and far;
He paints the wayside flower,
He lights the evening star;
The winds and waves obey Him,
By Him the birds are fed;
Much more to us, His children,
He gives our daily bread.

We thank Thee, then, O Father,
For all things bright and good,
The seedtime and the harvest,
Our life, our health, our food;
No gifts have we to offer,
For all Thy love imparts,
But that which Thou desirest,
Our humble, thankful hearts.

Matthias Claudius (1740–1815) was the son of a Lutheran pastor. Intending to go into the ministry, he attended Jena University where he was exposed to rationalistic influences which drove him away from his faith. He instead studied law and journalism. In 1777, a severe illness restored his faith at which time he began to write poetry and songs characterized by a strong devotion. In 1782, he wrote "Peasants' Song," a seventeen stanza song inspired by a harvest festival held by a Northern Germany farmer. The song was later published in shortened form and became extremely popular throughout Germany. "Peasants' Song" was translated into English by Jane M. Campbell and is today known as "We Plow the Fields, and Scatter."

Come, Ye Thankful People, Come

Come, ye thankful people, come,
Raise the song of harvest home;
All is safely gathered in,
Ere the winter storms begin;
God, our Maker, doth provide
For our wants to be supplied:
Come to God's own temple, come,
Raise the song of harvest home.

All the world is God's own field,
Fruit unto His praise to yield;
Wheat and tares together sown,
Unto joy or sorrow grown;
First the blade, and then the ear,
Then the full corn shall appear:
Lord of harvest, grant that we
Wholesome grain and pure may be.

For the Lord our God shall come,
And shall take His harvest home;
From His field shall in that day
All offenses purge away;
Give His angels charge at last
In the fire the tares to cast;
But the fruitful ears to store
In His garner evermore.

Even so, Lord, quickly come
To Thy final harvest home;
Gather Thou Thy people in,
Free from sorrow, free from sin;
There, forever purified, In Thy presence to abide:
Come, with all Thine Angels, come,
Raise the glorious harvest home. *Amen.*

Written by Henry Alford (1810–1871), this hymn was first published in 1844 in his Psalms and Hymns and also appeared in his Poetical Works in revised form. Following unauthorized revisions being published in other collections, Alford published his final authorized version in 1865. This familiar hymn is used frequently during the Thanksgiving season to celebrate the harvest, however it is important to note that the final three stanzas refer to God's harvest of his people.

Now Thank We All Our God

Now thank we all our God With hearts and hands and voices,
Who wondrous things hath done, In whom His world rejoices;
Who, from our mothers' arms, Hath blessed us on our way
With countless gifts of love, And still is ours today.

O may this bounteous God Through all our life be near us,
With ever joyful hearts And blessed peace to cheer us;
And keep us in his grace, And guide us when perplexed,
And free us from all ills In this world and the next.

All praise and thanks to God The Father now be given,
The Son, and Him who reigns With them in highest heaven,
The one eternal God, Whom earth and heaven adore;
For thus it was, is now, And shall be ever more. *Amen.*

From some of the severest human sufferings imaginable during the 30 Years' War in Europe (1618–1648), this great hymn of the church was born. Martin Rinkart (1586–1649) was called at the age of 31 to pastor the state Lutheran church in his native city of Eilenberg, Germany—the one city that became a refuge for those devastated by the war. He arrived there just as the dreadful bloodshed began, and there Rinkart spent the remaining 32 years of his life faithfully ministering to these needy people.

Prayers of Thanksgiving

Our Father who art in Heaven, we thank Thee for blessings, enjoyments, powers afforded unto us and unto all men, and for all good that has been given to this generation in its manifold forms. Help us to realize how many greater and better things God has waiting for us, and accordingly to glorify His name. *Amen.*

Once more we come, Lord, to the day of special thanksgiving. Our thoughts are turned backward. The days have rolled into the seasons, the seasons into the year. Each day has been crowded with Thee. Each season has brought forth new proofs of Thy loving fore-thought. May we this day pledge Thee our gratitude anew. Continue, we pray Thee, to surround us with Thy care. *Amen.*

We give Thee thanks, O Heavenly Father, for our food which Thou dost provide for us. Our thanksgiving could never measure up to Thy gifts, but we pray Thee to make us all more conscious of Thy blessed goodness, and help us to know Thyself. *Amen.*

Lord, behold our family here assembled. We thank Thee for this place in which we dwell; for the love that unites us; for the peace accorded us this day; for the hope with which we expect tomorrow; for the health, the work, the food, and the bright skies, that make our lives delightful; for our friends, in all parts of the earth, and our friendly helpers . . . Let Peace abound in our small company.

Robert Louis Stevenson

O Father, Thou Who Givest All

O Father, thou who givest all
The bounty of thy perfect love,
We thank thee that upon us fall
Such tender blessings from above.

We thank thee for the grace of home,
For mother's love and father's care:
For friends and teachers—all who come
Our joys and hopes and fears to share.

For eyes to see and ears to hear,
For hands to serve and arms to lift,
For shoulders broad and strong to bear,
For feet to run on errands swift.

For faith to conquer doubt and fear,
For love to answer every call,
For strength to do, and will to dare,
We thank thee, O thou Lord of all.

John Haynes Holmes

The Pilgrim Fathers

O God, beneath Thy guiding hand
Our exiled fathers crossed the sea;
And when they trod the wintry strand,
With prayer and psalm they worshiped Thee.

Thou heard'st, well pleased, the song, the prayer:
Thy blessing came; and still its power
Shall onward through all ages bear
The memory of that holy hour.

Laws, freedom, truth, and faith in God
Came with those exiles o'er the waves;
And where their pilgrim feet have trod,
The God they trusted guards their graves.

And here Thy name, O God of love,
Their children's children shall adore,
Till these eternal hills remove,
And spring adorns the earth no more.

Leonard Bacon

Thank you God for milk and bread,
and other things so good.
Thank you for those who help
to grow and cook our food.

Anonymous

O Lord, that lends me life, lend me
a heart replete with thankfulness!

William Shakespeare

A Poet's Grace

Before Meat
O thou, who kindly doth provide
For ev'ry creature's want!
We bless the God of Nature wide
For all Thy goodness lent.
And if it please Thee, heavenly Guide,
May never worse be sent,
But, whether granted or denied,
Lord, bless us with content.

After Meat
O Thou, in whom we live and move,
Who made the sea and shore,
Thy goodness constantly we prove,
And, grateful, would adore;
And, if it please Thee, Power above!
Still grant us with such store
The friend we trust, the fair we love,
And we desire no more.

Robert Burns

27

Recipes

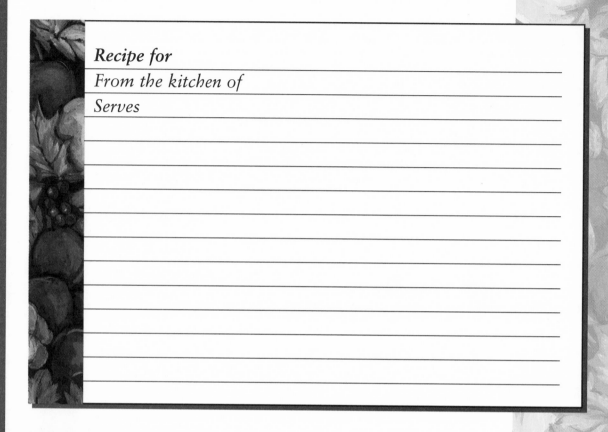

Recipe for
From the kitchen of
Serves

Recipe for
From the kitchen of
Serves

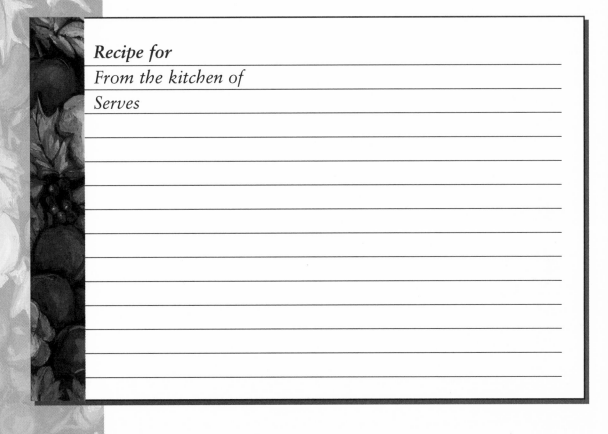

Recipe for

From the kitchen of

Serves

Recipe for

From the kitchen of

Serves

Recipes

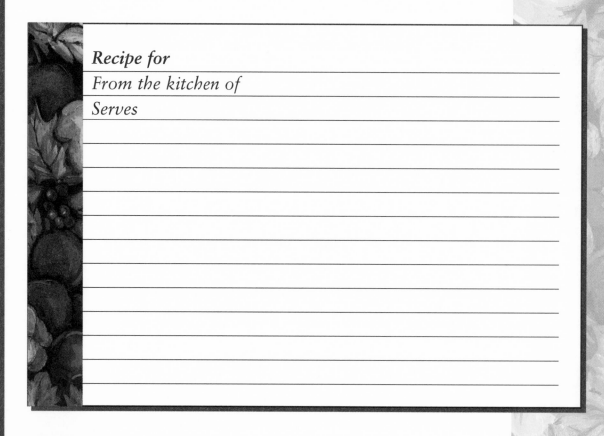

Recipe for
From the kitchen of
Serves

Recipe for
From the kitchen of
Serves

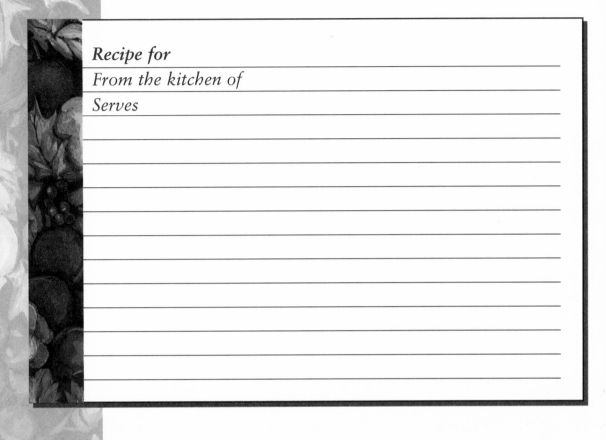

Recipe for

From the kitchen of

Serves

Recipe for

From the kitchen of

Serves

Our Annual Thanksgiving Memories

(Group photo here)

I thank my God every time
I remember you.

Philippians 1:3

Loved Ones Present at Our Thanksgiving Celebration

Giving Thanks

Name   I'm Thankful for . . .

_____

_____

_____

_____

_____

_____

_____

_____

_____

_____

_____

_____

_____

_____

_____

_____

_____

*(Pass the book around, allowing each person to record
what they are thankful for.)*

Name   *I'm Thankful for . . .*

On This Day

Our Thanksgiving Menu

_____

_____

_____

_____

_____

_____

Hometown news and world events this Thanksgiving Day

_____

_____

_____

_____

_____

_____

_____

_____

_____

_____

What was the weather like this year?

_____

_____

Conversations, Stories and Activities of this Thanksgiving

Hopes & Prayers

Hopes and Prayers for the Coming Year

_____

_____

_____

_____

_____

_____

_____

_____

_____

_____

_____

_____

_____

_____

_____

_____

_____

_____

_____

_____

Reflections

Other Reflections Upon this Thanksgiving Day

_____

_____

_____

_____

_____

_____

_____

_____

_____

_____

_____

_____

_____

_____

_____

_____

_____

_____

_____

Our Annual Thanksgiving Memories

(Group photo here)

Let the peace of Christ rule in your hearts, since as members of one body you were called to peace. And be thankful.

Colossians 3:15

Loved Ones Present at Our Thanksgiving Celebration

Giving Thanks

Name   I'm Thankful for . . .

_____

_____

_____

_____

_____

_____

_____

_____

_____

_____

_____

_____

_____

_____

_____

_____

_____

(Pass the book around, allowing each person to record what they are thankful for.)

Name   *I'm Thankful for . . .*

On This Day

Our Thanksgiving Menu

_____

_____

_____

_____

_____

_____

Hometown news and world events this Thanksgiving Day

_____

_____

_____

_____

_____

_____

_____

_____

_____

_____

_____

What was the weather like this year?

_____

_____

Conversations, Stories and Activities of this Thanksgiving

Hopes & Prayers

Hopes and Prayers for the Coming Year

Reflections

Other Reflections Upon this Thanksgiving Day

_____
_____
_____
_____
_____
_____
_____
_____
_____
_____
_____
_____
_____
_____
_____
_____
_____
_____

Our Annual Thanksgiving Memories

(Group photo here)

Give thanks unto the LORD, call on his name; make known among the nations what he has done.

1 Chronicles 16:8

Loved Ones Present at Our Thanksgiving Celebration

Giving Thanks

Name   I'm Thankful for . . .

_____

_____

_____

_____

_____

_____

_____

_____

_____

_____

_____

_____

_____

_____

_____

_____

_____

_____

*(Pass the book around, allowing each person to record
what they are thankful for.)*

Name   *I'm Thankful for . . .*

On This Day

Our Thanksgiving Menu

_____

_____

_____

_____

_____

_____

Hometown news and world events this Thanksgiving Day

_____

_____

_____

_____

_____

_____

_____

_____

_____

_____

_____

What was the weather like this year?

_____

_____

Conversations, Stories and Activities of this Thanksgiving

Hopes & Prayers

Hopes and Prayers for the Coming Year

_____
_____
_____
_____
_____
_____
_____
_____
_____
_____
_____
_____
_____
_____
_____
_____
_____
_____
_____
_____
_____

Reflections

Other Reflections Upon this Thanksgiving Day

_____

_____

_____

_____

_____

_____

_____

_____

_____

_____

_____

_____

_____

_____

_____

_____

_____

_____

_____

_____

_____

Our Annual Thanksgiving Memories

(Group photo here)

*I will give thanks to the
LORD because of his righteousness
and will sing praise to the name
of the LORD Most High.*

Psalm 7:17

Loved Ones Present at Our Thanksgiving Celebration

_____
_____
_____
_____
_____
_____
_____
_____
_____
_____
_____
_____
_____
_____
_____
_____
_____
_____
_____
_____

Giving Thanks

Name   I'm Thankful for . . .

_____

_____

_____

_____

_____

_____

_____

_____

_____

_____

_____

_____

_____

_____

_____

_____

_____

_____

_____

_____

_____

*(Pass the book around, allowing each person to record
what they are thankful for.)*

Name   I'm Thankful for . . .

On This Day

Our Thanksgiving Menu

_____

_____

_____

_____

_____

Hometown news and world events this Thanksgiving Day

_____

_____

_____

_____

_____

_____

_____

_____

_____

_____

What was the weather like this year?

_____

_____

Conversations, Stories and Activities of this Thanksgiving

Hopes & Prayers

Hopes and Prayers for the Coming Year

Reflections

Other Reflections Upon this Thanksgiving Day

_____
_____
_____
_____
_____
_____
_____
_____
_____
_____
_____
_____
_____
_____
_____
_____
_____
_____

Our Annual Thanksgiving Memories

(Group photo here)

Let us come before him with thanksgiving and extol him with music and song.

Psalm 95:2

Loved Ones Present at Our Thanksgiving Celebration

Giving Thanks

Name   I'm Thankful for . . .

_____

_____

_____

_____

_____

_____

_____

_____

_____

_____

_____

_____

_____

_____

_____

_____

_____

_____

*(Pass the book around, allowing each person to record
what they are thankful for.)*

Name   *I'm Thankful for . . .*

On This Day

Our Thanksgiving Menu

_____

_____

_____

_____

_____

_____

Hometown news and world events this Thanksgiving Day

_____

_____

_____

_____

_____

_____

_____

_____

_____

_____

What was the weather like this year?

_____

_____

Conversations, Stories and Activities of this Thanksgiving

Hopes & Prayers

Hopes and Prayers for the Coming Year

_____

_____

_____

_____

_____

_____

_____

_____

_____

_____

_____

_____

_____

_____

_____

_____

_____

_____

_____

_____

Reflections

Other Reflections Upon this Thanksgiving Day

Our Annual Thanksgiving Memories

(Group photo here)

*Enter his gates with thanksgiving
and his courts with praise; give
thanks to him and praise his name.*

Psalm 100:4

Loved Ones Present at Our Thanksgiving Celebration

Giving Thanks

Name   I'm Thankful for . . .

_____

_____

_____

_____

_____

_____

_____

_____

_____

_____

_____

_____

_____

_____

_____

_____

_____

*(Pass the book around, allowing each person to record
what they are thankful for.)*

Name   *I'm Thankful for . . .*

On This Day

Our Thanksgiving Menu

_____

_____

_____

_____

_____

_____

Hometown news and world events this Thanksgiving Day

_____

_____

_____

_____

_____

_____

_____

_____

_____

_____

_____

What was the weather like this year?

_____

_____

Conversations, Stories and Activities of this Thanksgiving

Hopes & Prayers

Hopes and Prayers for the Coming Year

_____

_____

_____

_____

_____

_____

_____

_____

_____

_____

_____

_____

_____

_____

_____

_____

_____

_____

_____

_____

Reflections

Other Reflections Upon this Thanksgiving Day

_____

_____

_____

_____

_____

_____

_____

_____

_____

_____

_____

_____

_____

_____

_____

_____

_____

_____

_____

Our Annual Thanksgiving Memories

(Group photo here)

O LORD my God, I will give you thanks forever.

Psalm 30:12

Loved Ones Present at Our Thanksgiving Celebration

_____
_____
_____
_____
_____
_____
_____
_____
_____
_____
_____
_____
_____
_____
_____
_____
_____
_____
_____

Giving Thanks

Name   I'm Thankful for . . .

_____

_____

_____

_____

_____

_____

_____

_____

_____

_____

_____

_____

_____

_____

_____

_____

_____

_____

*(Pass the book around, allowing each person to record
what they are thankful for.)*

Name   *I'm Thankful for . . .*

_____

_____

_____

_____

_____

_____

_____

_____

_____

_____

_____

_____

_____

_____

_____

_____

_____

On This Day

Our Thanksgiving Menu

_____

_____

_____

_____

_____

_____

Hometown news and world events this Thanksgiving Day

_____

_____

_____

_____

_____

_____

_____

_____

_____

_____

_____

_____

What was the weather like this year?

_____

_____

Conversations, Stories and Activities of this Thanksgiving

Hopes & Prayers

Hopes and Prayers for the Coming Year

_____

_____

_____

_____

_____

_____

_____

_____

_____

_____

_____

_____

_____

_____

_____

_____

_____

_____

Reflections

Other Reflections Upon this Thanksgiving Day

_____

_____

_____

_____

_____

_____

_____

_____

_____

_____

_____

_____

_____

_____

_____

_____

_____

_____

_____

_____

Our Annual Thanksgiving Memories

(Group photo here)

Give thanks to the LORD, for he is good; his love endures forever.

Psalm 107:1

Loved Ones Present at Our Thanksgiving Celebration

_____

_____

_____

_____

_____

_____

_____

_____

_____

_____

_____

_____

_____

_____

_____

_____

_____

_____

Giving Thanks

Name   I'm Thankful for . . .

_____

_____

_____

_____

_____

_____

_____

_____

_____

_____

_____

_____

_____

_____

_____

_____

_____

_____

(Pass the book around, allowing each person to record what they are thankful for.)

Name   *I'm Thankful for . . .*

On This Day

Our Thanksgiving Menu

_____

_____

_____

_____

_____

Hometown news and world events this Thanksgiving Day

_____

_____

_____

_____

_____

_____

_____

_____

_____

What was the weather like this year?

_____

_____

Conversations, Stories and Activities of this Thanksgiving

Hopes & Prayers

Hopes and Prayers for the Coming Year

_____

_____

_____

_____

_____

_____

_____

_____

_____

_____

_____

_____

_____

_____

_____

_____

_____

_____

Reflections

Other Reflections Upon this Thanksgiving Day

To him who is able to keep you from falling and to present you before his glorious presence without fault and with great joy—to the only God our Savior be glory, majesty, power and authority, through Jesus Christ our Lord, before all ages, now and forevermore! Amen.

Jude 24–25